LIVING IN
THE GRAY

LIVING IN
THE GRAY

a memoir by Katie Weber

atmosphere press

Published by Atmosphere Press

Cover design by Senhor Tocas

Atmospherepress.com

For my husband who I love dearly and who is my necessary.
And who puts up with me when I'm being completely unnecessary.

INTRODUCTION

Some of you likely already know this and if you do, you have author permission to skip this, if you want. For those of you who don't know, here's my deal: I'm a white lady in her 30s who has been fortunate to live a very blessed life. I grew up in a safe suburban town with good schools and a family who loves me. I am a cis-gendered, heterosexual person who is intelligent and athletic and who was told by others she was attractive, though my high school dating record says otherwise. I went to a nice, too-expensive college where I met my current husband who I now live with in Seattle and who I love dearly. By any token, I live a good and blessed life. Except, oh yeah, when I was 23, I got cancer. And then when I was 29, I had a relapse.

When I got cancer in my early 20s, it was definitely scary— I was so young, I was healthy, I ate well!—but I was FINE and the doctors were fairly certain I would have surgery and get treated and this would just be a blip on my radar! And I was fine, for almost 5 years! I went to Colombia and grad school and had jobs and was working on a career. My hair grew back and I loved to cycle and go dancing and walk as many places as I could. I remember wondering how or if I would tell my future children about it! Haaa, little did I know.

At 29, my cancer came back and I was NOT fine. It has affected my sight, my speech, my balance, and my appearance. There are many things I can no longer do, like dance or ride my bike, or walk everywhere. Hardest of all, while everyone around me is having babies or developing their careers, I'm sitting on the couch unable to do either.

So instead, I write.

I want to write a book like my first one with a cohesive theme and a snappy title that brings it all together, but my life feels a little too all over the place right now for that. My first book was about finding out you have cancer in your 20s and how that affects your life. And what you might need from the people around you. This book is more about my life now. Being 34 but not doing/able to do all of the things a 34-year-old typically does, like have kids & start a family or dive into a career. Many of my friends are doing these things, and don't get me wrong, NOT doing these things seems perfectly valid to me, but these are things I DEFINITELY wish I could do, but I can't. It's hard not to feel left behind or like you have nothing going on. I don't think anyone should stop living their lives or not share these things with me just so I feel better, I'm just saying, it's hard.

If you're looking for a book about cancer that's super inspirational and tells you everything is going to be okay, then this is not the book for you. This book is more about the reality of dealing with things that are not okay. In the cancer community, there is this term "sur-thriving" to talk about not only beating cancer, but also living your best life after it. This is my book about surviving but not necessarily "sur-thriving".

It turns out when you don't have a job or kids to distract you, you do a lot of thinking. Since I have neither of those, I've been forced to sit with my own existence and find things that give my life meaning, at least for me. This is not always an easy task and some days are better than others, but I'm alone and kinda bored a lot so I've been forced and given the opportunity to think about what really matters in life and what it means to live well.

I definitely don't have all of the answers and I know that living well looks different for everyone. I just have a lot of ideas and I like to write, so those ideas get put into words.

I'll try my best not to be too negative. After all, it is in my nature to always look on the bright side of life (I always sing Monty Python in my head when I hear that), but I DO plan to be real and if my realness makes you sad then, so be it. It IS sad. But not everyone can sur-thrive.

CHAPTER 1

The Truth, the Whole Truth, and Nothing but the Truth

You can't handle the truth! Oh wait, those two things are not related.

Anyway. I think you could use an update about my medical health right now. The facts, so to speak. I was on a chemotherapy regimen until 2019. I tried to find the exact date when I had my last dose of chemo, but I couldn't, so you'll just have to take my word for it. I decided to stop because it didn't seem to be having any effect on my cancer, but it WAS making me feel crappy. It didn't seem like a good trade-off, so I stopped. The only pills I currently take are Ritalin and Zoloft for my mental health (which I write about in a blog post entitled "Tools") and a multivitamin that contains Vitamin-D, because apparently, I live in Siberia where there's not enough sun and everyone is Vitamin-D deficient. I once had a doctor say to me, "Yeah, your Vitamin-D counts are kinda low, but they're not like Northwest low."

I still get MRIs regularly. What does this mean? It means that something most people don't have to do very often or ever is just a normal part of my life now. When you get brain cancer the first time, the scanning schedule goes something like this: for 3 years, you get scanned every 3 months. If you make it 3 years with a healthy scan, they go down to scanning you every 6 months, if you make it to 5 years, they scan you every year. If you make it to 10 years, they stop. I asked my doctor what the new schedule was and he said, "Oh, you? Yeah, we never stop scanning you." So there you have it. For the rest of my natural-born life, I will be getting an MRI.

They aren't the WORST thing—sure, they are loud and long and kind of annoying, but I've done them so many times that I'm kinda used to them. I know exactly what to wear (nothing magnetic!) and exactly what the pre-scan form asks (it's still green, by the way). I get MRIs so much that I can actually argue with the techs about what is allowed and what isn't. I don't actually argue with them, because I know that is annoying, but I still feel irritated when they make me do something that seems unnecessary.

They continue to scan me to hopefully confirm what has long been true: There's still an "aberration" on the images, but there seems to be no growth so I'm stable. AKA you might not be a martyr to this disease, but your life will still be crappy.

Not to get too dark, but that's the truth. Trust me, I know I'm lucky to be alive and all that. But being alive is so damn exhausting sometimes. I have double vision and dry-eye. I can't stand on my own. I can't walk on my own. This is because my ataxia is so bad that balance is not a thing I have. My hearing is bad, and I often have a hard time following a conversation, because my brain is real broken, so I can't always track what people are saying, and cognition is time-consuming. Talking isn't great either. I'm hard to understand, the quality of my voice is child-like, and my facial paralysis makes certain sounds hard/impossible to make. Plus, I have dry-mouth which can make certain sounds more difficult.

On top of all that, it takes me hours to eat and drink almost anything, no matter how soft or delicious it is. They say slow eating is good for you, but I don't think they meant THIS slow. I cough a lot when I drink. My stomach is really inconsistent, which makes trips to the bathroom either really urgent or hour-long affairs that ruin my schedule. Plus, my bathroom trips rarely produce the desired outcome.

To be a little bit of a Debbie-Downer, life is hard. That's already true, but most people have their full faculties to deal with that and they can distract themselves with a family or a job or a hobby. Which is why I titled this book *Living in the Gray,* because no one actually knows what's going on. Could this aberration be scar tissue? Sure. Could it be cancerous? Maybe. It's not really worth going in to find out (there's something for someone to invent: a way to test brain tissue that doesn't involve opening up the skull), so they'd rather keep an eye on it with fingers crossed.

You can see why I feel a little stuck. Sick, but not sick. Alive, but not alive. What's that saying? "If you want to make God laugh, show him your plans." Well, sorry God, but I won't be making you laugh anytime soon. (Cause I have no plans. They say a joke is really good when you have to spell it out.)

I'm not currently on any medication for my cancer. I get regular MRIs and I go to the doctor more than I would like. So, that's it. The truth, the whole truth, and nothing but the truth. As far as I, or anyone, knows it.

CHAPTER 2

Product Placement

I don't actually want to advertise anything (capitalism sure doesn't need my help), but the fact of the matter is that when you have as many problems as I have, you require a lot of products to just EXIST. Luckily for me, and people like me, there are a lot of products out there that make my life easier. So much so that when I can't find something I'm SURE exists because I need it so badly, I think to myself "oooh, what a good business opportunity," and then I remember that I know nothing about business and I'm lazy. I should give credit where credit is due and say that my husband, Will, has been instrumental in the finding and procurement of most of these items. It should be easier than it is, but it's not.

What are these products that make my life easier? Well, there are a lot, but I'll start with my shower chair. For most people, they just step into the shower to clean themselves, but for me, it's more of a production. Not only does my husband have to help me into the shower, but I also have to sit in a chair while I bathe. I've had a shower chair before—I tore my ACL in high school and had reconstructive surgery which required the use of a shower chair—but I've never had a shower chair like this. My shower chair has a backrest, two armrests, and it *moves*. This means I can put my legs either inside the tub or outside the tub. This also means that if push came to shove, I could get into the shower all by myself. The brand of this chair is Platinum Health and mine is bright blue. Like water maybe? One time, an occupational therapist saw my chair and was like, "That's awfully snazzy! Nice! I've never seen one like that before!" It begs the question, why, as an occupational therapist, is my shower chair new to you, but it also illustrates just how nice my shower chair is.

Another product that has proven really useful is the "Provail" cup. The reason that I have found this product so useful is that it only allows a little bit of liquid at a time. I need this, because my throat muscles are weak and if I drink too much thin liquid, I often cough (read: choke) and this cup keeps me from doing this. Most of the time. With the Provail cup, I'm also able to drink wine. This is especially important to me, because it makes me feel like a grown-up and not just a person using an adult sippy cup, but also because wine is delicious.

We've all seen grab bars in bathrooms (and I've got plenty of those!), but have you seen a grab bar in the middle of the room? Well, I have, and they allow me to stand up & down, get on & off my rowing machine, and dress myself. It is very useful when there's not a good wall nearby. My relationship with such a thing has been really love-hate (or hate-love, really). It offends my aesthetic sense: it's ugly, right in the middle of the room, and goes with nothing. It is generally an eyesore, but it allows me to do so many things I could not otherwise that I've grown to appreciate its existence. It's still ugly, though.

This will seem silly to people, but I have to espouse the wonders of the Revlon hair dryer that looks like a round brush. Because good ol' lefty (my left hand) is unreliable, I can't hold a brush while I dry my hair. We all know that a brush is how one gets their hair to look the way they want and that a brush while drying hair can create the volume and smoothness we all like and desire. Because I could not hold a brush, I just let my hair air-dry. This was all totally fine when I had really short hair without much to style. But my hair started to grow, as hair is wont to do, and it started air drying in all of these weird ways that I didn't much like. Enter the use of Revlon's One-step Volumizer hairdryer.

And you might be thinking what I thought, which was "It's just stupid hair, you don't have a job to go to anyway," and while some of that IS true—I don't have a job and it IS just hair—but hair is NOT stupid and not caring about my hair just because I wasn't going to a job implies that the only reason we ever care about what our hair looks like is 'cause of other people and I do not believe that to be true. So I decided to start drying my hair, and boy, I'm glad I did.

My hair looks nicer and fuller and like the hair of someone who tried! I'm not saying that anyone should do their hair because it's expected or that clean, styled hair is the only way to look professional or like you care, I'm just saying that for me, it made a world of difference to be able to have control over my hair and to be able to CHOOSE how I present to the world. Plus, I won't lie, it made me feel pretty again, which is a feeling, sick or not, disabled or not, we should all get to have.

The last product I will talk about is Lululemon clothes. I ended up with two of their items for free (Long story. Well, not really, just not an interesting one) and, yes, it is IN-CREDIBLY overpriced but it is very comfortable. Once they got over that whole "see-thru legging" thing, it seems like they became a brand that really does sell nice things. There are other brands that are way cheaper and also sell nice things (might I suggest the brand "A New Day", available at Target and generally delightful?), but I gotta give credit where credit is due and admit that my free Lulu Lemon leggings are probably my favorite. That being said, I recently checked some out on their website and I refuse to buy them because why are they so expensive??

I don't just want to be a shill for some products, so what's my bigger point here? My point is that, disabled or not, we all need a little help from time to time. Coming to terms with needing help is NO easy thing (and to say I've come to terms with it is VERY generous), but I've learned that resisting help when we need it only makes things harder. For some people, this help is something tangible, a product like a shower chair or special cup. For some people, it's less tangible, like "me" time or meditation or a massage. And for some people, it's a shoulder to cry on, a text in the middle of the night, or kind words from a friend. For most of us, it's some combination of all three.

So, figure out where and how you need help and don't be afraid to ask for it. And when you hear about a good brand of time machine, let me know.

CHAPTER 3

Choosy Moms Choose Jif

I need to flesh this out, but it's something I think about: the connection between choice and freedom. To be free means getting to make our own choices. To choose where to work, who to marry, whether or not to wear a mask (wait, I think I disagree with my own point here), and how we live our lives. I think that's why arranged marriage can seem so icky: the lack of choice.

After what my illness has done to me, I feel like I have a lot fewer choices. There are some things I just CAN'T do, the only choice I always have is HOW I think about things.

Now, I'm not suggesting that everyone who finds themselves in a tough situation is just thinking about it wrong or that a bad situation will be okay if you just think about it differently. That's neither true nor fair. I'm just saying that with such limited choices, it was liberating to realize that HOW I think about things is one of them.

There's not much in life we actually do control, but we like to think we do. We like to believe that our choices affect where we end up and how things go for us. To some extent, this is true, but there are many things that are just completely out of our control and no matter what we do, we don't avoid them. For example, cancer is not something we choose (at least I think/hope not, because it's awful), and it often leaves fewer choices in its wake. We can't help but wonder, DID I choose this? Is this some sort of retribution for a bad decision I've made? Sometimes I wonder if I could have made a different choice that would not lead me to brain cancer, but I'm not sure things work like that...

Choice and control are ALWAYS interesting things to think about in life, but especially now, given the pandemic (I could probably talk about abortion and lots of other hot-button political issues when it comes to choice but I don't really want to open THAT can of worms), because many people are choosing not to get vaccinated. Now, I'm not a scientist and I can definitely understand how certain people are afraid of government & medicine, but from my understanding, getting everyone vaccinated is our best shot against Covid. I know there are all sorts of questions about the vaccine and that new variations keep showing up, but there is overwhelming evidence that vaccinated people are less likely to DIE, and I feel like that should be enough to just get vaccinated. Yet there are a lot of people out there who CHOOSE to not and feel like the government mandates go against freedom of choice. But who are you making that choice for? Is it just for you? Most of our choices aren't. To pretend that we live in isolation and that our choices don't affect others is to live in naivety. I'm a huge believer in the social contract, and I feel like if you CHOOSE to live among other people, you are agreeing to the idea that your choices should reflect what's going to be the best for everyone.

Choice and control are big issues in the cancer community, and it's because cancer makes you feel like you control nothing. Does having cancer mean I'm less free? I might say yes. I don't mean in like the legal sense—I don't think anyone can arrest me for not having a job, and other than revocation of my license (which is probably actually safer for everyone), there is no law that says I have to be in a wheelchair. But am I free to just walk out the door and go hang at the coffee shop? No, I'm not. Not safely, at least.

So does choosing to think about things differently become less of a choice if it's the only choice you have?

I'm trying to find the blessings in this illness. To CHOOSE to look at it in a different way, but that's not always very easy. There's this famous quote that really resonates with me right now: "The right choice and the easy choice aren't always the same thing."

CHAPTER 4

'Til Death Do Us Part

I could write a whole book on relationship stuff (and there are certainly people who do!), because my illness has changed both me and my husband, Will, so much. We are both learning a ton every day—sometimes the same things, sometimes different things, and sometimes contradictory things—and this illness has surely left ME grappling with my identity, but it has also left us grappling with the identity of our relationship.

There is no RIGHT way to go through hardship together, just like there is no right way to have a relationship (granting that autonomy and joy are part of the relationship). One of the AMAZING and maddening things about a relationship is that everyone needs different things. There is no RIGHT or WRONG way to be a partner and we can't be inside everyone else's relationship. Despite all of that, I do think that one thing is true across all relationships, and that is communication. You need to be able to talk to your partner honestly and directly, and when they are honest and direct with you, you need to be able to hear them. I have had to learn all of this and I still need to practice it, because I can be really passive-aggressive (many women are because we are taught early on that direct aggression is not for us), and I can let my feelings get hurt when Will is direct with me.

I know "communication" is like the cliché thing and the obvious relationship advice that everyone gives, but it's cliché and obvious for a reason: it's REALLY FUCKING IMPORTANT.

Will and I were together for nearly a decade before we tied the knot, so we weren't exactly terrible communicators in the first place. We already had a pretty strong relationship, but my illness and dependency on him for EVERYTHING means that sometimes, communication is a matter of life and death, safety and danger.

Or a matter of whether I pee my pants or not.

We rely a lot on metaphor to help us communicate and understand each other. I read a book once where the author uses the metaphor of "spoons" as a way to talk about her emotional capacity or overall ability to "deal" at that moment, so Will and I talk about spoons all of the time. For example, Will said to me once "you wake up every morning with zero spoons, but you somehow still seem to pull them out of nowhere." This was very sweet and I knew exactly what he was talking about. We were recently searching for a metaphor for times when we are in a good mood and more receptive, so maybe the other person can complain more or express their frustration more readily. The metaphor we landed on was turning up or down our music. Like, "I'm in a good mood right now so it will be easier for me to turn down my music". For example, the other day, I had a doctor's appointment, and I'm generally in a pretty good mood when I have an appointment. As I wrote about in my post "safe spaces", the hospital is a good place for me. For another, it's a day entirely focused on me and my well-being: Will drives me to my appointment, we usually get coffee out, and the nurses and doctors are there to see ME. I was able to say to Will "Today is a good day for me to turn down my music," and he knew exactly what I was saying.

Speaking of metaphor, spoons are in short supply for us. There are many days when they all get used up. And just like there is a little spoon and big spoon, there are two kinds of spoons for us: the caretaker spoon and the husband spoon (the cancer spoon and the relationship spoon). Sure, we want to wake up with a drawer filled with an equal number of both spoon types, but that isn't always the case. Sometimes the drawer is completely empty and sometimes, there are only big spoons. Will said one time that he feels like he's 70% caretaker and 30% husband, so in spoon-speak, he is 70% big spoon and 30% little spoon. The ideal is probably 50/50, but sometimes, it's just not there.

When Will is feeling 70/30, it's hard for me not to feel 70/30. Like 70% of me is cancer and a lot to deal with, and 30% of me is the person that is maybe worth dealing with.

We are working on this and some days are closer to 50/50 than other days, but I guess that's just how it goes: meandering along, trying to make one another happy while staying happy yourself. Some days are easier than others to remember why you're with that person in the first place.

This is pretty silly, but I think it is a CRUCIAL lesson for anyone who is disabled or sick and in a relationship. It took a TV show for me to really get it, and though I know it, it's very easy for me to forget about it. I was watching a TV show where one of the characters has a miscarriage. She is obviously really sad, and her husband says something to her like "You know, I lost a baby, too. I'm part of this and I also get to be sad."

I'm not comparing my situation to the horrors of miscarriage, but it took that for me to realize, "This is Will's life, too." Sure, cancer affects me differently than it affects him, but like most things, no one is ever actually alone. For me and for Will, gone are some of the trips we were hoping to take. Gone is the family we wanted to raise together. Gone, in many ways, is the wife he fell in love with. One time, I said to Will, "I can accept a smaller life for me but not for you," and his sweet response was, "This IS life."

Even though Will and I probably go through a lifetime of struggle every day, that's what partnership IS, right? Choosy moms choose Jif, and I CHOOSE Will, and every day, no matter how many spoons he has, I have to (get to?) choose him again.

---

*if you are experiencing domestic abuse or feel like you are in an unsafe relationship, please call the national hotline at **1-800-799-SAFE (7233)***

CHAPTER 5

Community
(and not the show, though it's a good one so you should watch it if you haven't seen it)

As I think I've made clear, I try to focus on the GOOD things about my shituation, and when I do that, I can't help but think of all the people I've met or the relationships I've been able to deepen just by being available a LOT.

When I think about times I've felt really happy versus times I've felt really sad, community is always at the heart. People coming together over a shared interest or shared activity often means that you find them, or find something in common with them, when you otherwise would not. If you see someone as part of your community, you're more likely to take care of that person. So yeah, community is pretty important.

I've very much resisted being part of the cancer community—I really didn't want to identify as a cancer victim or be pitied. But then I realized that, guess what? Identify or don't identify, my life has been unquestionably changed by cancer and not identifying with it meant I missed out on a lot of great resources—and people. So I joined the community, the young adult cancer community. It's one of the shittiest communities to be a part of that's made up of some of the least shitty people.

I'll start with Cancer Lifeline's (CLL) YA support group. One thing I think is really special about CLL is that, while so many orgs/hospitals understandably look at the PHYSICAL effects of cancer, CLL thinks about and offers support for some of the other things like identity and connection and hobbies. I've met some really awesome people through this support group, and it feels really nice to talk to a group that I don't have to explain anything to. I'm not undergoing any active treatment, so I'm not always going through the same things they are, but I probably HAVE been through those things, and I'm so glad a community exists for young adults with cancer. Like I've said, there aren't a lot of cancer groups for young people out there and it's just different from being older and getting cancer! Plus, I've made some really good friends, including one who is coming over this week and another who has the same "rare" type of brain cancer as I do AND is from the northwest Chicago suburbs (the coincidences don't end there but for your sake, I'll end there)!

Through this support group, I got connected to CLL and was able to donate 50% of the proceeds from my first book to them (which I plan to do again with this book) and have taken advantage of some of their other offerings. Through my donation, I also got to meet the executive director and participate in their annual fundraiser. I don't know the E.D. very well, but I can tell you that he is a lovely person filled with kindness and curiosity.

Another connection I've made through having cancer is with my disabled rowing team, Seize the Oar (STO). If you knew me, you knew I was one of those annoying people who actually like to work out (working out gives you endorphins and endorphins make you happy!). In shaping my new identity, I knew that being active would have to be part of it. I was doing videos on YouTube, but that wasn't cutting it (sorry

Coach Kozack and Claudia), so I did some internet research and found STO. Balance is my main issue, so I figured rowing would be a good thing to try, and I'm sure glad I did!

Because of the delightful pandemic, we haven't been able to spend a lot of time in the water, but STO hooked me up with an awesome erg to borrow at home, and every Sunday, I have been participating in their virtual practices which always include rowing and some kind of strength activity. I can't say I'm good at rowing, but I love water and I love learning about a physical challenge that's new to me. I have to say that my favorite part about being active has always been the team aspect and the opportunity to get to know new people. Rowing has been really individualistic for me, so I can't wait to explore some of the more collaborative aspects of the sport.

That being said, though I don't know the other participants well, the two "coaches" are really great people to whom I feel connected. It's not the athletic community I had come to know, but I'm sure that community is there, and just because you're disabled, it doesn't mean you're not hella strong.

I know social media has a lot of evils and we probably won't know its effects—both good and bad—for years, but I would be remiss if I didn't talk about my use of social media in a chapter about community. Usually, when people write about social media, they talk about the bad things, but I'm going to talk about some of the good things. Having lots of free time and a pretty rare disease, I rely on social media quite a bit for entertainment and connection. I am part of every medulloblastoma group on Facebook and Facebook helped me find Stupid Cancer, an organization focused on young adult cancer, and I have relied on these groups and this org for connection and information.

Plus, social media allows me to see the world from my couch! Yes, so do books and podcasts and stories, but social media allows me to see the people that I love doing cool things (which hurts sometimes but is mostly just great). And since I love to write and writing is my best opportunity to express myself, social media allows me to connect with people in a way that allows me to feel more like myself. Behind a computer screen, I don't have cancer and I'm not in a wheelchair.

For a very long time, I avoided leaning into the cancer community, and then I realized how important community is to me and that I'm not going to be able to build community in the way I had before. I am a cancer patient, there are others like me who understand, and refusing to identify as one was just pushing me farther and farther away from those people.

CHAPTER 6

Divine Providence

I wrote about my feelings on religion and God in my first book in a chapter called "How I Found Jesus Through Cancer" and I think I made it pretty clear that I don't really know, but "God" and religion are not really part of my spirituality, so I don't know if I believe in "divine providence." There are definitely some eerie coincidences, though. I recently made Will watch *Say Anything* with me, because I have always loved it, and he had never seen it. I had totally forgotten, but it takes place in Seattle. And then a bunch of my college friends were from the Pacific Northwest. So could you say that Seattle and I were fated, or do we just find fate in the coincidences of everyday life?

I do know that we now have a dog that, Will and I like to say, came to us by divine providence. What do we mean by that? What feels like a long time ago (it was probably like 2019), I expressed the desire to hang out with an animal, but we didn't feel ready to get a pet (like a dog; Will is deathly allergic to cats—such a shame, he's so great in most ways) because they are a LOT of work. A friend of ours had a friend who owned a dog that just sat around while she was at work.

Voila, a match made in heaven!

Our very kind friend would go pick up the dog, bring him to our place to hang out (read: cuddle), then our VERY kind friend would come pick him up. Enter into our life: Javi.

Javi is brown, and cute, and small, and mostly very well-behaved, but not when it comes to a very important thing: children. So when his owner got pregnant and asked us if we wanted to take him (I can't imagine why she didn't want to conduct that fun experiment), we said yes.

So now we have Javi. He is a rescue pup so his age and breed are not certain, but we think he's like 5 years old and a Chauweenie which is, apparently, a combination of a Chihuahua and Dachshund. We can't be sure, but this is exactly what he looks like, so close enough. He has floppy ears that feel like velvet, and he sleeps A LOT (and that's coming from someone who once slept until 4 in the afternoon). He doesn't care about tricks or balls and he barks surprisingly loudly at our neighbors and anyone delivering things to us. I've tried to teach him to fetch, but he just doesn't care. He's probably not the dog I would choose, but he's the dog I have so... divine providence, right?

Luckily, he has been the source of much entertainment for Will and me, and though I know it's more work for Will, taking Javi on walks is good for him AND he gets to be Javi's favorite person by being in charge of his food. Plus, the love and amusement he expresses toward Javi is so cute, I think it's worth it.

I grew up with cats, but Will didn't grow up with pets (save for a bird named Jake who I better mention before I'm single), so I hope that Javi gives him the "pet itch" and he realizes that a house is not a home without a pet. I have to remind myself that he's just a dog and doesn't play favorites (not that dogs can't like certain people more, just that there isn't really such a thing as "Javi doesn't like me!").

I think part of my insecurity is not being the ones to choose and train Javi, but I know that he will not live forever and we can't just rely on divine providence or random intervention if we want a dog in the future.

CHAPTER 7

If Wishes Were Fishes

My mom has all these great sayings from her Aunt Libby (my great-aunt), and one of those sayings is "If wishes were fishes oh how I could swim!" Meaning, of course, that I have so many wishes that if they were fish, I could swim really fast. I know the logistics don't really add up, but that's not the point of a saying and you get the general idea.

There are so many things that I wish were different, and I've definitely wasted time perfecting my list for the genie when he shows up (I wish I could swim again, I wish I could kiss again, I wish I could talk more easily and clearly... or is it I wish...? ...okay, perfect might be a lie) I think it's human to wish for things, and I guess the key is to know when a wish is a wish and not to let your wishes run your life.

I used to do this thing where I would think "Well, if only WHATEVER and everything will be fine," and then whatever would happen, and everything would not be fine. So there are a couple of takeaways from this that I see: 1) The idea that, if you expect nothing, you'll never be disappointed; Or 2) Wishes are exactly that—wishes—and they cannot fix everything.

I think there's something to be said for takeaway number

one, though I think it's sad. It's good for us to temper our expectations and have realistic ones. For example, I no longer let myself believe "If X, then Y", but I think wishes/expectations are part of what keeps us going and trying. If I didn't wish I could swim again, would I be looking for ways to make that safely possible? Would my sweet husband help me into the water at the beach even though it was a lot of work for him and he was terrified I would drown? No.

Sure, I have to accept that I'll probably never jump off the pier in Door County into Lake Michigan like I used to or that I won't likely swim out in Lake Washington until I can see Mt. Rainier again, but I don't think the wish is the problem. I think the problem is that we think that wish needs to look a certain way. We have to be willing to change our idea of how that wish comes true. I had a yoga teacher once who was also an actor and he did some silly video for Amazon. I, being full of tact, asked him what his endgame was with acting. He said, "Sure, it would be nice to become rich and famous, but I just love to act, so I'll take any gig that pays, because it means I get to act." I loved that, because so many of us (me included), just don't do something if it doesn't look exactly how we envisioned it. I don't think that anyone should "settle", I just think that, sometimes, it's possible to get to the heart of a wish if we re-envision what fulfillment looks like.

CHAPTER 8

The "New Normal"

Can I write a book in 2022 and not mention the pandemic? I don't think so. There are a lot of vaccinated people now and hopefully we'll be out on the other side soon, but a return to normalcy? Doubtful. We will probably still eat in restaurants and see movies and hug our friends, but I really don't think the world will look like it did before. I hope it actually looks better and that we learn some lessons about what life COULD be and what ACTUALLY matters to us.

For instance, I'm interested to see how certain companies convince their employees to go into the office full time. I mean, I know actual face time is valuable, but I also know a lot of people who aren't exactly missing their commute! And who can argue with less traffic?!

I also hope that this shows us that we need one another. I don't know about you, but I just missed people (well, most of them). I missed the energy of people buzzing about or going to a restaurant for dinner. I missed hugs! The other day, I actually HUGGED somebody and it felt so good! Even being able to feel someone's gross elbow skin is a privilege. (I don't actually do that and I don't think you should, I'm just saying, touch is rare.)

I think, above all, the pandemic showed us what's possible and how flexible we can be. Can't go to school? Okay, we'll offer some classes online. Can't be in choir? Don't worry, some really talented musician will make something happen. I'm not saying online school or creative choirs are BETTER than being in person, I just think the pandemic gives us the opportunity to CHOOSE what we bring back and what we don't.

One thing I hope sticks around is the slowness and the chance it gave people to just chill out. I won't lie, as excited as I am for people to get social again, I'm nervous, too. The pandemic created a weird world, but I was less weird in it. Pandemic life felt more like my life but for everyone. Fear for your health? Check. Cooped up inside and not going out? Check. Not able to attend or throw a large gathering? Check. Life was moving at a slower, albeit infuriating, pace. It felt easier for me to keep up.

With Covid, I experienced a lot less FOMO or actual MO than I had previously because there was nothing to miss out on. I'm very glad that my friends and loved ones will experience a lot less anxiety, I'm just afraid of getting left behind.

Choice seems to be a big thing with the pandemic and in life. We can never be totally certain what we actually choose and what we don't—so many of the things that feel like a choice have been heavily influenced over time by peers, media, society—but the pandemic provides a real opportunity to actually see what choices we make. Sure, some choices will be made out of necessity, but I do think we are in a unique position to CHOOSE what serves us and what doesn't.

CHAPTER 9

Art and Legacy

A friend of mine once said, "The things we create are all that's left of us when we go." She is a singer and creates beautiful music, and what she said really got me thinking about art and our legacy. Would anyone talk about William Shakespeare without his sonnets or his plays? Maybe, but we wouldn't be able to see the world through his eyes or know how he would put something (plus, the English language would lack so many expressions! What would we do?!).

This is all pretty convenient to say for someone who is CREATING a book and prides herself in being able to write in her own voice, but art gets shit on a lot. Like, what can it be USED for or what is it GOOD for? As if bringing color and joy to the world isn't good enough! As art programs get stripped from schools and curricula across the country, maybe a more concrete answer is needed to that question. What is art good for? It's good for creating a legacy, that's what it's good for.

I never expected to write a second book—the people that mattered liked my first one, and I was able to donate a bunch of money to CLL—but then I realized that I'm in such a different space than when I wrote that first book. I thought I'd get to be one of the lucky ones, one of the "sur-thrivers", but I was not. To call this life "sur-thriving" would be an overstatement. Every day is hard, and my quality of life involves a lot of silver linings and perspective shifts.

There are certainly good times, and there are people that I love and laugh with, but is this the life I wanted? Do I get to do the things I was hoping to do? Nope. I may not be being treated for cancer right now, but to pretend that my life hasn't been forever changed by cancer is doing a disservice to me and everyone around me. I know that life never goes as planned and that we have to be willing to change our expectations, but I was already a pretty flexible/chill person. I don't think I needed all of this to help me understand that you can't always get what you want!

I'm writing this book for many reasons. One, I love to write and if the hospital is a safe space for me, so is the blank page. When I write, I get to say exactly what I want to say, I don't have to interrupt anyone, and I don't have to deal with anyone saying "what?" or "I didn't understand you." Two, I don't want ANYONE to EVER feel alone because they can't do what everyone else is doing. Lastly, as you know, I'm always trying to look on the bright side of things, so if anything good can come of my war with cancer, it's books.

I hope this art does what some of the best art does: connects to the human experience and tells someone they aren't alone. That's cool if this becomes part of my legacy, but if it doesn't, and there's one less person out there who feels alone in their sentiment, then so be it. That's enough.

CHAPTER 10

Blog Posts

As you likely know, I regularly write in a blog to help me process my feelings. Writing is when I feel most like me and I find it easier to talk about things through writing. My posts are basically just about whatever I feel like writing about, but I feel like some of them are uniquely suited for this book, especially some of the more recent ones. I know it's kinda cheating to just re-print some blog posts, but I did write them and I promise I edited them! (Though just a little bit, because I want them to reflect exactly where I was in that moment.) Plus, at my editor's wise suggestion, I added some commentary to many posts. So, here they are, some relevant blog posts to living in the gray right now.

....

It Is What It Is
6/30/21

A friend of mine recently told me that he and his spouse are getting a divorce. I guess this shouldn't have shocked me given that the divorce rate is like 50%, but you always want to believe that you and your friends will beat the odds and they are both such delightful people, I was sure they would figure it out. I was searching for the right thing to say and I just kept coming back to "It is what it is."

I've always hated that expression—it seemed so defeatist to me, like why even try?!—but as I've gotten older, I understand why it's become so popular. Sometimes things just suck and that's all there is to it (and I know a little bit about sucky situations).

What if that phrase wasn't defeatist but just necessary? When I was younger, I thought everything could be fixed. So, what did that mean? It meant it was my job to fix it. Or that something could be done to set things right. But maybe there are things that can't be fixed. Maybe they are just broken, and trying to fix them leaves us like Sisyphus, pushing that heavy boulder up a hill.

By accepting that there are some things that can't be fixed, I don't think we're saying a thing isn't SAD, I think we're saying that there's no real way to make it UNsad. We can take all of that energy we expend pushing that boulder up the hill and apply it to something that actually makes us happy.

Because sometimes, it just is what it is.

2022 commentary: I'm reading this now and still getting the defeatist vibe: like, things just suck and the sooner we accept that, the better. While I do think that's PARTIALLY true—there are some things that can't be fixed that we just need to accept—but even when things suck, I think there ARE things to be done that will make things better. This is probably not the best comparison, so please forgive me, but what if all of the Freedom Fighters who marched across that bridge in Alabama had just said, "It is what it is," and moved on? I have to remind myself of this daily. I cannot undo cancer or get back to who I was before, but that doesn't mean I can't do ANYTHING. In fact, I planned my first trip without Will to my best friend's bachelorette party in Palm Springs. Sure, I'm a little nervous and it requires more planning than it would have in the past, but it's not impossible. Yes, there are certain things that are what they are, but that's not a good reason to give up entirely.

....

Intention
6/26/21

"DRIVE WITH INTENTION!!!" is something I used to scream a lot at Seattle drivers (within the confines of the car, I become the meanest person—we all do this, right?). Seattle/Washington drivers don't seem to care if they get where they're going or not. And I'm not talking about driving style like aggression or passivity. I'm talking like basic driving stuff, like not noticing that a light has turned green or taking so long to take a turn that it causes me to miss the light. It used to make me BANANAS (and probably still would, I just don't drive anymore).

It's funny because for all this talk about driving with intention, I sure don't always LIVE with it. I tend to just let things happen and react as I see fit.

In a lot of ways, this makes sense. To someone who got cancer in her 20s, plans can seem pretty stupid. Some plans ARE stupid and God IS laughing, but a little planning gets us going. It can be motivating.

I was just at home in Arlington Heights and then we went to Will's childhood home in Massachusetts, where his parents still live. My parents are selling their home, all of my closest friends from childhood/high school live in the Chicago area and 3 of them just bought houses, Will's parents have done a TON of work on the house and it looks nicer than it has in years (I think Will would agree with me on that, so I can say it), and we hung out with one of Will's high school buddies and his AWESOME wife and adorable son at their cute home. It's hard not to fantasize about living in the Chicago area or Massachusetts, but would I like that? I don't know.

I think that's part of the problem—we are at a threshold where we have to choose—be intentional about—what's next for us. I think that is made even more difficult by the choice constraints that we face—my health, career, family. There is no obvious place for us to settle down. We'll just have to be really INTENTIONAL about where we go next.

2022 commentary: This one is pretty easy to respond to, because I'm writing this from the couch in my new HOME that Will and I decided to purchase in October. In many ways, this house sort of fell into our laps, but I LOVE it and we had to be intentional about deciding to start looking to buy. As you probably well know, there are a lot of variables outside of your control when buying a house, so there had to be a fair amount of reacting, especially in the crazy Seattle housing market, but we did DECIDE to stay in Seattle and we did DECIDE that we really liked this house. I'm trying to live my life with a bit more intention these days. It's easy for me to forget that my choices do matter and that sometimes, things only get done if you decide to do them.

. . . .

Toolbox
5/25/21

Recently, I wasn't on top of it and let my prescription for Ritalin lapse. It's considered addictive and you have to get a new prescription every month so you really have to be vigilant. And I wasn't. This meant that my mood was pretty low. I don't have ADD; I take Ritalin to give me an energy boost and a mood boost, because anyone who knows me at all knows that my life is pretty hard and exhausting.

I'm not a stranger to anti-depressants and I don't think anyone should be ashamed of taking them, poor physical health or not, because life is hard and sometimes our chemistry isn't exactly right to deal with it. That said, I don't like to be on a pill to not feel depressed. I said to Will today, "If you need a pill to feel okay about your life, that's not a good sign." When I took antidepressants before, I wanted to get off of them as quickly as I could, because it felt like a false sense of happiness. I wanted to build up my own toolbox to fight off my demons.

So I did. I wrote in a journal. I exercised a lot. I did yoga. I ate well. I read and did things that nourished me. And it worked. Sure, we all have our ups and downs, but overall, when I was unnaturally down, I could turn to my toolbox.

Nowadays, not only is my life a lot harder, but my toolbox is pretty empty. I'm trying to fill it up with new hobbies and new exercises and new ways to elevate me when I feel deflated, but the tools I have don't always work.

In regards to my Ritalin need, Will said, "You know, some of us just need a little extra help," and I thought that was sweet. I thought about it in terms of the toolbox. The medicine is just another tool since some of the other tools aren't in there right now. It's kinda like being handed a Phillips-head screw, turning to your toolbox, and seeing you only have a Flathead screwdriver.

Ritalin is my Phillips-head screwdriver.

2022 commentary: One tool I don't mention that I think is a really important one is distraction. Many people have jobs or kids to keep them busy and distracted. They are not forced to think about the mundanity of the day to day, because they're already too busy thinking about that expense report or little Timmy's potty-training schedule. Not that there are not plenty of good reasons to have children other than to distract you from the futility of life, just to say that when you're already trying to keep your child alive or make sure their clothes are presentable enough for the public, you know what your purpose is. You live your purpose! You don't have to think about the sad things as much, because you are distracted. I'm not necessarily saying this is a good or bad thing, just that we distract ourselves in our lives partially to avoid sitting in the uncomfortableness. That's where entertainment comes from!

••••

The Strength in the Sad
3/11/21

"I wish I could do [x]," or "Man, it sucks that I can't do [y]." If I had a dime for every time I said or thought one of those things... well, I wouldn't be rich, but I'd have a lot of dimes. I think it's very human to want what we can't have, but I think it's also very human to act like we are happy all of the time.

I definitely fall into this trap, because I want to be perceived as "strong" at every turn. Instead of looking at all of the things I CAN'T do because of cancer, I try to look at what I CAN do. I'm so afraid of becoming a downer or of being that "sad cancer patient" that everyone pities. It's easier to just tell everyone, including myself, that I'm happy.

But guess what? I'm over it. I'm sad and things are hard, and I hate that having cancer has meant that there are so many things I won't get to do. And I'm working on believing it myself, but I also want to acknowledge that there is strength in admitting that you're sad. Especially in our culture which puts such an emphasis on being happy.

Admitting that you're sad requires a certain amount of vulnerability and authenticity that is scary. Admitting to your true feelings may feel a bit like admitting to your weaknesses, and we want to pretend like no one sees our flaws and that we're simply heroic, and we tend to think that no one will relate to our sadness, but I think that's very false. I think the hard things are very much what make us human and relatable. I think, or at least I hope, that heroes can get sad sometimes, too.

I have to remind myself of this, because I can get so caught up in being "inspirational," like if this shitty thing is going to happen, I might as well prove how unaffected I am by it all! But, recently, I have felt less like finding the blessings and the lessons in it all. Trying to find meaning in it makes it feel kind of like it was "supposed" to happen or something.

I think it's okay, and even strong, to admit that yes, this sucks, and sometimes (all of the time) life's not fair. Authenticity takes vulnerability and vulnerability takes strength. I can see why expressions like "it is what it is" are so popular: sometimes things just suck and there's nothing we can do about it. The only thing I've thought to do about it is not to let myself get stuck in the sad. It's okay to be sad sometimes and to feel sad about things that are sad! But we can't always be sad. For the number of things that make me sad each week, there's as many, if not more, that inspire me. Without sadness there is no happiness, and that's just not worth it.

So yeah, I'm sad that I'll never be pregnant and that I won't have my own classroom and that I'll never climb Mt. Kilimanjaro (it was one of my life goals). That IS sad! Admitting that doesn't make me weaker, it makes me real.

2022 commentary: I don't have much to add to this, because I agree with it. In a society that is so likely to sweep things under the rug, I think it DOES take strength to tell it like it is. It's interesting that I invoke the phrase "it is what it is", given my aversion to it, but the matter-of-factness of this saying is not my problem with it. I don't think it's WEAK to admit when things are not what you'd like. As I've said a few times, "when your reality looks like mine, realism and pessimism can look awfully similar." So, it is what it is, and sometimes what it is sucks, and it's okay not to pretend it doesn't.

....

Enough
2/12/21

I'm part of a young adult cancer support group, and this past weekend, we had a yoga teacher lead us in a yoga nidra session, and one thing she asked was, "What's that mean thing you say to yourself all of the time?" For me, it was that I'm not enough. Enough what? Enough of an activist? A baker? A friend? A wife? We all want to be everything, but we can't. At least most of us can't.

I'm not trying to suggest that we can't do whatever we put our minds to or that we don't do a lot—many of us do more than we give ourselves credit for—but I am saying that something's gotta give, and that maybe "enough" is what you're already doing.

Or maybe that's just what I'm telling myself so I can feel like I'm trying. Either way, I don't think we are really, truly aware of our efforts.

We also can't know what we are to other people. In the same way that I see other people and think to myself, "How do they do it?", maybe there are people out there who see me and think the same thing. We can never know how complete we seem to other people or how much other people need us to feel complete.

This is definitely something I want to work on, this feeling of not being enough. It's funny, because when it comes to health things, I'm definitely like, "Ok, enough."

····

The Little Things
1/17/21 & 4/30/21

We've all heard that expression "it's about the little things" but it truly is. When I think about some of the things I miss the most, they are so small. Sure, I miss many of the big things— driving, my hair, a career—but in many ways, those things seem obvious. It is the smaller things that we don't think about that we long to do again. For me, it is taking my favorite pair of boots to the cobbler to be resoled or re-heeled. Or picking out the perfect mug for my hot coffee. Or standing in the shampoo aisle at the drugstore for far too long, just smelling all of the bottles of shampoo. So silly. So trivial. Yet so important.

Another little thing that is hard or, in this case, that I just don't do, is laundry. I know that laundry is like the Lambchop of chores (the chore that never ends), but when you don't do your own laundry, it's hard to keep track of your clean clothes. Don't get me wrong, Will does a fantastic job with the laundry, I'm just kind of a control freak and have a little bit of trouble just handing my clothes over to someone else. (For some context, when I started doing my own laundry, it wasn't because anyone told me I HAD to, it was because I WANTED to be responsible for my own socks).

I often don't realize I miss a little thing until I hear someone else talking about it like it's no big deal. And it's NOT. That's the point. I once heard that when the country is in a recession, sales of expensive nail polish go up because people need a way to treat themselves without spending TOO much money. This, to me, is paying attention to the little things: spending more money than you would normally but still only spending like $8, because it brings you joy, if even for a moment. It's not huge, but it's something.

Big stuff doesn't come around that much so we need the little things to keep us going, because sometimes, the little things are all we have. I'm sure I'm not alone in taking these things for granted, so the next time you bound down the stairs to grab something you forgot or jot a quick note as you run out the door, take a second to recognize that action and be grateful for the fact that the little things are still little for you.

2022 commentary: It's definitely important to appreciate the little things and there definitely are little things that I miss, but I think the big things are having more of an impact on me than I'd like to admit. Lately, I've been thinking about the big thing of having a child. While, in some ways, it's nice to have that decision made for me—I mean, what kind of future would I be giving a child? I know, I know, every generation has their struggles and worries for the future, but I might argue that climate change is different. I can't really know, because I didn't live in the past, but at least before all of the problems were OF earth and the problem wasn't that we're slowly killing earth. Anyway, it was kind of nice to not have to agonize over that decision and it certainly made our house search easier, because we didn't have to consider school districts, but I LOVE kids and I had all sorts of ideas about the kind of mom I wanted to be and I don't get to do that. Plus, the way many adult women make their friends is either through their job or their kids. Not to say that there aren't other ways for me to make friends, just to say that's another obvious path that's gone.

The other path, as mentioned, is a job. I know that, to many, I'm lucky to not have to work, and believe me, I am so grateful that I still get to be alive and buy doughnuts without a job, but working is something I ENJOYED. I like to use my mind and to solve problems. I like routines and inside jokes. Most of all, I liked feeling like I had an impact on the world and thinking about how to make the world a better place, even if for only one person. My career was in education and I really do think schools are the intersection of and the answer to all of the ills of our society. I enjoyed thinking about all of that and being right in the middle of everything that was going on. Not that I don't still think about it, because I definitely do, but it's just different when you're right in it. I don't get to do that anymore.

Kids and a career are BIG things that I definitely miss. I don't know if I'll ever stop missing them.

••••

Happy-medium
11/8/20

This is a topic I've been thinking about for a while and I'm fairly certain I already did a post on walking the line, and while I think they are similar concepts, I think finding a happy medium is more about finding a place to sit and stay, and when you are walking the line, you are (hopefully) mainly focused on not falling.

I am in a YA cancer support group and we were sort of talking about this subject in relation to identifying as a cancer survivor but not wanting to just be seen as a cancer survivor. Like, I want people to know why I can't smile, or why I'm in a wheelchair, or why it takes me hours to eat, but I don't want to be pitied or have people adjust their expectations just because they "feel bad." I found myself asking the group, "What's the happy medium there?"

When I was in college, there was this coffee shop called "Middle Ground" and I think its title took on many meanings. One was simply practical: it was located smack dab in the middle of campus. Another was cutesy: you drink coffee at Middle Ground and you grind coffee. And then, I think, the less talked about meaning, is that it's a place where a lot of conversations happen, and how else do you find the middle option?

I think humans are always calibrating towards the middle. This, I think, could be one explanation for the world's extreme lean towards liberalism or conservatism. Common sense tells us that what we probably want is somewhere between the two, but we're not really sure where that is, so we try one way, and instead of slowly correcting until we reach a good spot, we over-correct and end up going really far the other way.

I think the only way to not over-correct is to have a lot of different ways to do things. When you draw a line (freehand) it's hard to go from point A to point B and keep the line straight. But if you're going from A to F with all sorts of other points between, it's a lot easier to get there with a straight line. I think the same is true with conversation.

The more seats at the table, the more voices in the conversation, the better and richer the conversation will be. I believe that the better a conversation is, the easier a path to the happy medium will be.

<u>2022 commentary:</u> I'm not entirely sure where I heard this, but a politician said, "We've all heard that saying 'we just need more seats at the table' and I would say, actually, we need a whole new table." I'm not sure how this relates to finding a happy medium, except to say that, sometimes, maybe a happy medium isn't enough.

••••

Ego
9/11/20

I've been doing this sketching challenge with my mother-in-law where we picked an object that we have to sketch/draw daily. We have chosen a tree. We text each other photos of our creations, and at the end of the challenge (one month), we will send each other our drawings. Part of it is accountability, giving one another a reason to do the drawing. Part of it is to practice letting other people see your (sometimes not what you wanted) art. And part of it is that it's just fun!

The other day, my MIL said something to me like, "It was just that old ego getting in the way again," and it got me thinking a lot about the ego.

I think we so often relate the ego to vanity but they are not the same thing. I feel like my ego is strongest and loudest in things that have nothing or little to do with my appearance. For example, every time I try to do something I've never done, like make a new meal, and I apologize for it maybe being bad and qualify it with, "Well, I've never made this before," that's just the ego talking. I'm scared to look bad so I try to pre-empt any criticism that others might have when, really, others are just glad to have a meal made for them and totally don't expect it to be top-notch.

It also made me think about where ego can be helpful. We've all met someone who apologizes too much (women are more likely to do this, FYI) which is super annoying, or won't say what they want to eat, for fear of dictating where the whole group gets food. Instead, they silently tolerate their taco when what they REALLY wanted was a hamburger. These people likely have no ego. This is when a little ego is helpful. That feeling of, "I am important. I have every right to be here. My preferences matter." It's an important thing to have.

I was thinking about this a lot in relation to my new reality. I have been so focused on the things I can't do anymore and how to find the right replacement that I didn't develop new things to do.

Some of the things I used to do were fun and I liked them and I would like to continue doing them, but I think a big part of my hesitance has been my ego. I've been feeling embarrassed about not being able to do what I used to do and needing to modify things to make them work for me. My ego keeps me from asking for help when I need it, and it means that I'm actually able to do LESS than I could otherwise.

But my ego is also the thing that gets me out of bed every day. It's what brought me to my chemo appointments. And it's what keeps me writing.

So that's just another thing to work on: balancing the ego. Because that's what I and we all need: more to work on.

2022 commentary: Vanity and ego? Can we talk about that? I recently decided that I shouldn't give up all notion of vanity just because I don't get out much or because it's hard for me. I was looking at old photos and I had this thought, "Dang! I was pretty!" I basically never think this about myself anymore. Sure, there's a part of me that thinks it's pretty egotistical to look at yourself and think, "I'm so pretty!" (Unless you're playing Maria in West Side Story), but I do think that's an important part of our ego—to be feelin' ourselves. I wrote a post on self-love (which you can read here in a sec), and self-love is really important. The ego is necessary for that.

····

Broken Record
8/11/20

I have really been wanting to write a post lately, because writing is my sanctuary and I've been feeling very forlorn these days, but then everything I could think of just made me feel like a broken record: my struggles are all the same and I'm always grappling with the same stuff, and I kind of feel like I've already said what I can say on some things.

I imagine that a lot of us feel like broken records these days. If we are fortunate enough to be working from home, our home is both our office and where we sleep at night. "I don't work from home, I live at work!" I've heard a lot of people talking about how they don't know what day of the week it is, because every day is just the same. I hate to say, "Welcome to my world," but welcome to my world!

Maybe it's like anything, and it's just how you look at it. It's just perspective.

Some days, it's a lot easier to find the perspective that makes something seem good, but it's there.

Speaking of broken records, one of my favorite songs that I've been listening to lately is 'Into the Mystic' by Van Morrison. If you've never heard it or it's been a while, you should really listen to it, because Van Morrison has a beautiful voice. If you disagree, then I'm sorry. I just don't share your perspective.

2022 commentary: I imagine that, these days, we can all relate to this more than ever. We had that brief moment when we thought we were free from the virus and that things could go back to like before (a friend recently called it our "summer of love" and I thought that was great) and then there was Delta and Omicron and numbers started rising again, so we retreated to our dark little corners to hide again. This meant less going out and fewer adventures, and therefore, fewer opportunities for stories. I think everyone is feeling a bit weary of pandemic life, but guess what? That IS my life, and I don't think my summer of love is coming any time soon.

....

Safe spaces
6/17/20

I had to have a small surgery yesterday (don't worry, I am FINE), and it brought me to the hospital and I realized something kinda messed up: the hospital is a safe space for me.

What is a safe space? It's a place where you feel relaxed and accepted. You know all the rules, and you feel like, in that space, you can be who you need to be at that moment. For many people, home is a safe space and it should be. It's comfortable and filled with all of your things that you chose, you know the rules, and it's often filled with your favorite people. For some people, home is not safe. It signifies an abusive spouse or an abusive parent. If that is you, please contact an organization that can help you, because no one should ever feel unsafe in their own home.

Hospitals feel safe to me because I know all of the rules. Everyone is very nice to me and is paid to be there and get me things. I can be my best self: strong, patient, and nice. Most of all, I don't stick out like a sore thumb. Mostly everyone there is sick, too. A nurse can know my medical history just from a glance at my chart. I don't have to explain myself. Sure, the pokes and prods are annoying, and I wonder how many times I can repeat my birthday before I go crazy, but like I said before, these things just provide proof of how strong and patient I can be! Most people rightly dread going to the hospital, but I don't hate it. What does that say about me? What does that say about my life?

Everyone should have a safe space, a place they can go and feel at ease and be properly seen and heard, no matter how they act. Ideally, this safe space has people you trust, and ideally, you have more than one safe space.

Right now, feeling safe and finding a place to feel that way is probably more important than ever. If we are not stuck in our homes., we are stuck somewhere. The safer a place is, the less stuck we may feel.

Domestic abuse hotline: 800-799-7233

2022 commentary: I touch on this, but I'm realizing now more than ever how true this is. Safe spaces, for me, are mostly about people. Like, my home, for instance, feels most like a safe space when it's got people I love in it. Hospitals are a safe space for me, because everyone takes care of me and I know all of the rules, but also, people in hospitals are just NICE. It's just a place to be where there are lots of caring people. Not everyone is a caring person, but the hospital seems to have more of them than the general world does. The kinder the people, the more likely they are to treat you with respect. For me, being treated with respect makes me feel safe. I feel the safest when I'm comfortable and that's more about who's in the room than the room that we are in.

···· ·

Both sides now
6/7/2020

Growing up, my parents always told us that bad situations were opportunities to learn, often calling them "lessons." At some point, when my brother was young, something bad happened to him and he said, exasperatingly, "Not another lesson." He was done trying to find educational opportunities in the bad things.

He was done with it, and maybe I should start with it. I've been thinking about my illness through the lens of it as a taker. Cancer is certainly a dirty little thief. As Sufjan says in his song about cancer that I listen to a lot (and probably shouldn't), it "takes and it takes and it takes."

It takes childhoods and futures and lives (both literally and metaphorically). Personally, it has taken a lot: my career, my smile, my independence (just to name a few). I could name all of the things cancer has taken from me until I'm blue in the face, but it has also given me a lot.

It has given me the opportunity to know a lot of kind and interesting and inspiring people. It has taught me so much about the medical world. It has given me the chance to see people for who they really are, especially my husband who doesn't get it right 100% of the time, but tries damn hard and is willing to learn alongside me. Shit, cancer gave me my book and this blog which was/is a joy to write.

And, sure, bad situations are a shitty way to learn. That's why my brother was so exasperated when he said that to my parents. "Not another lesson." And I recognize how much this sort of sounds like "bad things happen for a reason," or "it's all part of God's plan," but I promise you, no. Sometimes I think bad things are just bad and there is no plan, as much as we wish there were. I just know that being angry all of the time hasn't been helping me. I've been focused so much on all of the things that cancer has taken away from me, I think it's time to focus on what it's giving me. Otherwise, I'm just going to stay stuck in the bad.

Some days, it's easier to have this insight than others. Some days I feel very much like my brother did when he was young. "Not another lesson." But what if I choose to look at my life differently? Then what?

2022 commentary: This book is largely about finding the good things in the bad, and I am very good at that. My Godmother once said of me, "You could give Katie a piece of shit as a present and she'd still write you a nice thank you note." I think she was commenting more on the fact that I'm good about writing thank you notes, but I think it also speaks to my ability to find the good things in stuff. I don't think it is a bad way to live life, but it is fucking exhausting. And that's the truth: I am exhausted. Yes, it's better to look at the things I've been given through this, but sometimes, I just wanna whine and be sad about everything. And eat pastries.

· · · ·

Patience
5/24/20

I'm not particularly religious and I know it has been over-read at weddings, but I found myself turning to this today:

Love is patient, love is kind. It does not envy, it does not boast, it is not proud. It does not dishonor others, it is not self-seeking, it is not easily angered, it keeps no record of wrongs. Love does not delight in evil but rejoices with the truth. It always protects, always trusts, always hopes, always perseveres.

I think we think about this idea a lot when loving others, but what about when loving ourselves?

There are certain aspects of that passage that stick out to me more than others. One is, "it keeps no record of wrongs." The reason that stands out to me is that I am very competitive and I like to be "right." I like to win. Who doesn't? The flip side of that is, in order to win, someone has to lose, and in our lives, we lose plenty! I think the trick is seeing losses as learning opportunities rather than marking them off as more evidence against why you are not worthy of time, of success, of love.

Another reason this part sticks out to me is because I let myself have a lot of regrets. I'm not good at reminding myself that there's nothing I can do about it now and moving on! We all know that hindsight is 20/20 and it's easy to look back on something and wish we had done it differently, but I have to remind myself that we all just do the best we can in that moment. Regrets are silly and I KNOW that but I still let myself have lots of them.

The other part that really got my attention is the patience part. I am not always a patient person, with myself especially. I want everything to happen NOW. I like to think this is one reason I don't really like long-distance running—it takes so LONG (and it's boring and I suck at it and it hurts). Like most people, I want instant results. This is why microwaves and TV shows that release all of their seasons at once and the shake weight are so popular (was the shake weight popular or just funny?): it's 'cause we want results yesterday. Our society values fast and I was definitely a product of that: I talked fast, walked fast, and typed fast. A lot of this stuff was really great and I miss it, but it did not make me a very patient person.

Now I am slooooow and everything takes a long time. I need more patience just to get by, but I also need to be patient with myself. I spent like 30 years getting used to doing things one way, it's going to take some time to get used to doing things differently. After like 30 years I was still working on self-love, so sure, it's easy for me to look back on my old self and see all of the things I liked, but I have to remember that, even when I had those things, I didn't always see them.

So let's all remember to be gentle and patient with ourselves, because self-love is patient. Self-love is kind.

CHAPTER 11

The Gray

I titled this book *Living in the Gray* because my life feels really gray right now. Am I a cancer survivor? Sort of. Am I a cancer patient? Sometimes. Do they know or understand what's going on inside of my head? Nope. Few things in life are actually black and white (Oreos, Othello, old photos just to name a few) but most of us have other things going on that require organization or distract us from the absurdity of life, but not me. I don't have those distractions so I get to think a LOT.

I totally understand why humans want to make things black and white, yes and no. We want a clear indication of where to go, because living in the gray is HARD. And filled with lots of uncertainty. We've all gotten better at dealing with uncertainty with the pandemic, but we still know that it doesn't feel good.

People often call the United States a "melting pot" and while there are a lot of valid criticisms of that term, I think the idea behind it is right. You can live in Seattle and get great Indian food. You can live in Chicago and eat good barbecue. Where does all the best stuff happen? In the gray. What happens when you melt black and white together? You get gray. That's another reason I titled this book *Living in the Gray,* because it's hard but it can also be great.

When things are black and white there are only 2 choices. When things are gray, there are a lot of different choices. Sure, choosing is more difficult, but you are also more likely to choose something you're happy with.

It's kind of odd that, as someone who feels like so many choices have been taken from her, I would choose to name my book after something that symbolizes multiple choices to me. I guess because, though I'm forced to live with uncertainty, we all are, we just don't often have to stare it in the face quite as much as I do. The gray is something we all need to get comfortable with because uncertainty is the only thing we can ever be certain of.

I may have fewer choices, but one thing my husband reminded me of is that there might be fewer paths, but there is a path through the gray that I'm not choosing to take. A path where I give up and throw in the towel because everything is so hard and why try anyway when we have no idea what's ahead? I don't choose that path. I choose the path that sees me getting up every day and trying. Trying to have new experiences and trying to make choices that will bring me joy and happiness.

ACKNOWLEDGMENTS

Everyone at Atmosphere Press that helped me to make this book a reality. My parents, who always supported me and made sure I was well-educated. Specifically my dad for being my de facto lawyer in this process. My blog followers who encourage me to write and prove to me that there IS an audience out there for my crap. Last, but certainly not least, my husband, Will, without whom my very life isn't possible.

ABOUT ATMOSPHERE PRESS

Atmosphere Press is an independent, full-service publisher for excellent books in all genres and for all audiences. Learn more about what we do at atmospherepress.com.

We encourage you to check out some of Atmosphere's latest releases, which are available at Amazon.com and via order from your local bookstore:

Dancing with David, a novel by Siegfried Johnson

The Friendship Quilts, a novel by June Calender

My Significant Nobody, a novel by Stevie D. Parker

Nine Days, a novel by Judy Lannon

Shining New Testament: The Cloning of Jay Christ, a novel by Cliff Williamson

Shadows of Robyst, a novel by K. E. Maroudas

Home Within a Landscape, a novel by Alexey L. Kovalev

Motherhood, a novel by Siamak Vakili

Death, The Pharmacist, a novel by D. Ike Horst

Mystery of the Lost Years, a novel by Bobby J. Bixler

Bone Deep Bonds, a novel by B. G. Arnold

Terriers in the Jungle, a novel by Georja Umano

Into the Emerald Dream, a novel by Autumn Allen

His Name Was Ellis, a novel by Joseph Libonati

The Cup, a novel by D. P. Hardwick

The Empathy Academy, a novel by Dustin Grinnell

Tholocco's Wake, a novel by W. W. VanOverbeke

Dying to Live, a novel by Barbara Macpherson Reyelts

Looking for Lawson, a novel by Mark Kirby

ABOUT THE AUTHOR

Kathleen (Katie) Weber was born in Arlington Heights, IL (a suburb of Chicago) and now lives in Seattle, WA. When she was 23, she was diagnosed with rare brain cancer (only 400 people in the U.S. are diagnosed with it every year) and spent almost five years without it, thinking it would just be a weird thing that happened to her that she'd tell her kids about some day. She had jobs in education, went to grad school, traveled to Colombia, and got married! But guess what? The cancer came back and with a vengeance! She is now wheelchair-bound and unemployed and lives in a cute house with her even cuter husband and dog.

FOL

AUG 2 6 2023

Made in the USA
Monee, IL
15 July 2022